NATIONAL
GEOGRAPHIC

Cotton Comes From Plants

Norman Yu

We wear many types of clothes. We wear t-shirts, hats, and shorts. These kinds of clothes are often made from cotton.

Cotton comes from cotton plants.
Cotton plants grow seed pods full
of fluffy, white cotton.
How does the cotton on a plant
become the cotton that we wear?

Each cotton plant grows
many seed pods.

Each seed pod has fluffy, white cotton inside.

5

Farmers pick the cotton.
This is called harvesting.
What happens to the cotton next?

Farmers use a machine
called a cotton picker
to harvest the cotton.

The cotton is sent to a factory.
Machines clean the cotton.
The clean cotton is sent to
a spinning mill.

This machine fluffs the cotton
and removes the dirt.

There, the cotton is combed.
Combing makes the cotton straight and smooth.
A machine twists the straight, smooth cotton to make yarn.
The yarn is long, thin, and strong.

At a spinning mill, a machine twists the cotton into yarn.

Now the yarn can be woven. Large machines called looms weave the cotton into fabric. Then the fabric is sent to a clothing factory.

Looms weave the yarn into large pieces of fabric.

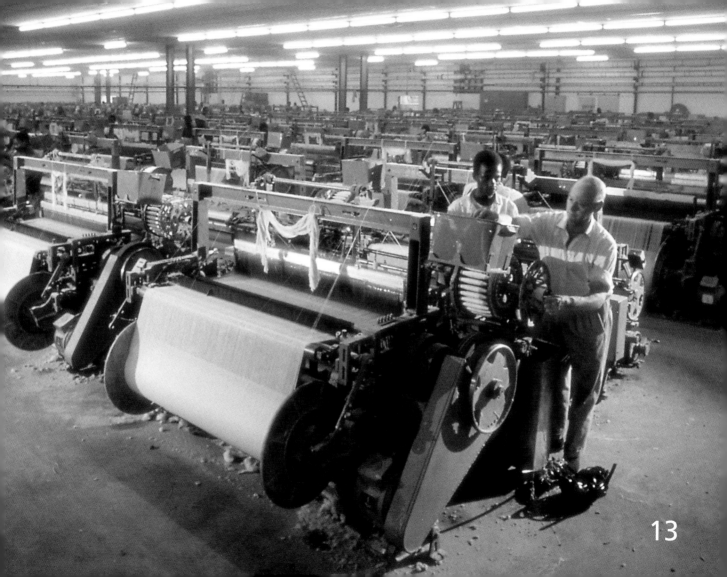

People sew the fabric into clothes.
They make clothes such as
t-shirts, hats, shorts, and dresses.

People use sewing machines
to sew fabric together.

Now the cotton is ready for us to wear!